Where I Found My Joy

M.J Manning

Balboa Press books may be ordered through booksellers or by contacting:

Balboa Press
A Division of Hay House
1663 Liberty Drive
Bloomington, IN 47403
www.balboapress.com.au
1 (877) 407-4847

Interior Graphics/Art Credit: M J Manning

ISBN: 978-1-5043-2110-5 (sc)
ISBN: 978-1-5043-2111-2 (e)

Print information available on the last page.

Balboa Press rev. date: 03/11/2020

BALBOA.PRESS
A DIVISION OF HAY HOUSE

One sunny day a little boy named JJ woke feeling some of his Joy was missing,

So off he went to look for it.

He checked in his toy box, Red Rob the robot Teddy Bear and his beach ball,

But no Joy...

Next he crawled under his bed, Goldie bear, the sock Mum was looking for, and "AHH CHOO!" lots of dust,

But no Joy...

He decided to look in the fridge, ham, cheese, eggs "Mmmm" yummy chocolate cheesecake!

But no Joy…

Suddenly he had an idea and raced outside to look in Peppers kennel,

JOY! But not his Joy…

He checked behind his favourite apple tree,

No Joy...

He was having fun looking so he went back inside and peered behind the television,

No Joy…

It was getting late so his Mum asked him to put on his PJs and brush his teeth.

He got his toothbrush out and looked in the bathroom cabinet,

No Joy...

He felt his Joy was somewhere near so he brushed his teeth and thought I'll keep looking tomorrow.

And then, just as he had given up, as he put his toothbrush away, there it was His Joy!

Right where it has been the whole time, within him, supporting and inspiring him every day!

Printed in the United States
By Bookmasters